GENTLE ON MY MIND

A slow, sensitive approach to recovery from mental
illness

Sandra Coniam

To my much loved and loving family

Introduction

Mental illness appears to be recognised by successive governments, at long last, as a medical priority which needs addressing – not least because it seems to be rapidly becoming an epidemic, with one in four of us now being affected, to a greater or lesser extent. Young people, even at primary school age, are starting to display symptoms of acute emotional stress and, partly because we generally live longer now, Alzheimer's disease and other forms of dementia are becoming increasingly prevalent at the end of our lives.

Of course, this inevitably means that more financial resources will be needed to support those who are suffering but there can be no doubt that society as a whole would feel safer and there would be less funding needed for prisons, for example, if mental illness were not allowed to progress unchecked. More than that, we now have the opportunity to try to **understand**, in a more open way, the circumstances which can contribute towards people, of whatever age, from whatever lifestyle, from whatever background and of otherwise apparent overall good health, to feel that there is no hope, and even **(in the very worst case scenarios)** no alternative, to contemplating ending their lives. The stigma once attached to the sufferer is being slowly but surely eroded as more and more of us succumb to the crushing symptoms of this debilitating illness. Each discussion, which now takes place fairly regularly in the media, hopefully makes it easier for someone to open up and say, '**I** need help.' There is still a long way to go, however. If a colleague is absent from work due to a virus, for example, it is often openly spoken about, as opposed to the hush hush manner in which sickness from a mental disorder is kept as confidential as possible.

It is as though we are trying to be protective, anticipating that our colleague may feel that their illness is something to be ashamed of, whereas the more we accept that this illness can happen to **anybody**, the more this attitude will change.

There are different forms of depression. They include:

Re-active depression – triggered by a traumatic or stressful event

Dysthymia – continuous mild depression that lasts for over two years. Sometimes called persistent depressive disorder or chronic depression.

Manic depression/Bipolar disorder – a mental health condition that causes extreme mood swings. The main symptoms of bipolar disorder are episodes of extreme highs and lows which can last for several weeks.

I am writing this book as someone who has witnessed the symptoms of severe depression at first hand and subsequently made some study of the subject. It is an attempt to try to help both the person who may be so frightened by the way they are feeling at the present time and/or someone who is observing a loved one showing acute signs of distress and hopelessness. For someone who has never experienced mental illness themselves, to see someone they love laid so low by an illness that they may not understand can be overwhelming – the desperation of wanting to help, alongside a complete feeling of helplessness and inadequacy, can be a devastating experience in itself.

Severe depression can be as equally debilitating a condition as some of our worst feared medical conditions. After all, how often does one hear the expression 'it's mind over matter' when it comes to the question of using positivity to try to at least minimise the effects of our illnesses. However, in the case of clinical depression, there is no logic, no mental stamina, no hope, faith or whatever else we may sometimes summon to our aid with varying degrees of success, **when it is the brain itself that is sick.**

We find it difficult to understand the correlation between the brain and the mind. The brain is a biological organ in the same way as our heart or our liver but its complexity separates us from every other living organism on the planet. Its functions control not just the very tools of our everyday life, such as movement, but also the less conscious processes which can affect our thoughts, mood swings, memory, creativity and imagination. It produces chemicals which can influence our way of feeling at any given time – one example being serotonin which is often referred to as the 'happy' chemical. Equally, external situations, stimulants or chemicals such as drink, drugs, even prescribed medications such as antibiotics can, on occasions, produce involuntary 'nightmarish' reactions from the brain. Certainly, an acute lack of sleep **alone** can have a major effect on our mental health. Sleep deprivation is known to have been used very effectively as a method of torture, such is the acknowledged resultant devastation to body and mind.

Intensive 'over thinking' and having an overactive, analytical mind means that your brain is racing when it is time to sleep. You turn in on yourself and become very self-critical. Some people will tell you that they live with very little sleep and have done all their life, managing this situation without it inevitably resulting in depression. But a good night's sleep is a precious commodity – we may not realise just how precious, until and if we find ourselves deprived of it over a long period. The severity of its effects then manifests itself in our day to day life.

Physical tiredness resulting in exhaustion can be accompanied by alarming reactions like hallucinations, violent nightmares, a feeling of aggression, irritability and what can appear to be a complete change of personality. Likewise, damage to the brain as a result of a stroke can change a patient's personality in some cases. It is no great revelation, therefore, to understand to just what extent the health of our brain can affect our personality.

If the sufferer perceives their problem to be the result of some spiritual (even demonic) power at work, there may be added terror, which is why it is imperative that the **trained mental professional is consulted urgently**.

There are now very effective drugs which can be prescribed to alleviate the **symptoms** of acute mental disorder, giving the patient relief from the feeling of panic and lack of control whilst enabling the professional to assess what may have led to the patient's current state of mind and to make an initial diagnosis with a plan of effective long-term treatment. The medication may take two or three weeks to build up in the body before the patient feels a noticeable improvement. Some patients may believe that what has happened to them is a result of fate and that it was destined, therefore, that a spiritual being is in control of their mind. If this **were** the case it may be helpful (once they are able to think more clearly) for the sufferer to consider that far from being out of control and irreversible, **man-made** medication can be such an effective antidote to their worst mental experiences. Modern antidepressant drugs do not come with the added worry of addiction, which used to be the case in the past, and treatments like Cognitive Behavioural Therapy (CBT) can give long term relief and hope, helping us to acquire the skills needed to manage our mental health much better in the future.

Mental illness is, in my opinion, a **physical illness**, in the same way as (albeit very different from) other physical illnesses and it occurs when the brain, the computer filing system of our experiences and thoughts

- becomes overwhelmed and shuts down as a defence mechanism in order to rest.

It **demands** that we rest. We are not at peace in some way and we need rest first before being able to personally diagnose, with help, what may have led us to our current low emotional state, so that we can move forward again in our life. The longer we have tried to hold on without asking for help, the more intense the experience. The deeper the pit we have dug, the longer it takes to dig our way out again. It cannot be rushed and must, with resolve, take its course.

Perhaps I should say here that it may be easier in some cases to identify the trigger for the onset of depression – a bereavement, for example, or homelessness, a recent handicap or post-traumatic stress disorder which has forced an adjustment to our life.

It may be the loss of a job, respect, dignity; it could be financial problems or the departure of our offspring who are setting off to lead their own lives. These are just a few of life's potential changes which can affect us immensely and they can be major challenges to most of us – we don't always know what is around the corner and may not have been able to, or even thought about trying to, prepare ourselves for some of them. Perhaps you do not feel there are enough hours in the day – you have so many demands on your time and there is never enough time for you. There are skilled, empathetic counsellors who may be able to help you with whatever is making your life oppressive or overwhelmingly sad, such as bereavement counsellors and professionals who are trained to help steer us through many of life's pitfalls. Look for information at your doctor's surgery, or contact an independent financial adviser or Age UK (a charity which supports the elderly population in Britain) if the anxiety of making major decisions in later life is causing stress and pressure, especially if you are on your own.

But how about those of us who feel that our illness cannot be related to any of those above and who therefore add guilt to our burden, as there is 'no excuse' for feeling this way? Apart from professional help there are excellent books available which you can read in the privacy of your own home, offering invaluable advice as to how to approach a myriad of life's problems.

Cognitive Behavioural Therapy will help you gradually and consistently lose that harmful feeling of guilt. It helps you to realise that your illogical, negative, harmful thoughts are not exclusive to yourself as you are encouraged to follow a pathway out of your maze of thoughts to a clearer view once more.

The first priority is to take small steps towards recovering enough to be able to awake ready to at least try to face each day, instead of feeling you are unable to drag yourself out of bed.

Then as you gradually improve, you can set about focussing on what choices you have available and what mental and practical help you can source in order to be able to change or adapt the areas of your life which are proving to be so painful to you, and which prevent you from leading a calm and tranquil life. Even in today's often manic society, there may be some areas of your lifestyle which could be changed, or adapted at least.

If you feel that this is impossible, acceptance will be necessary, but **learned** acceptance, achieved by way of a change in your thought processes. It might only require a temporary acceptance with an opportunity to change your situation at a later stage.

This book is aiming merely to offer **hope** to sufferers of depression and their loved ones and as a straw to clutch whilst striving to find the way to **look forward once more and to find some meaning in life. The ability to take pleasure in the things in life which can bring us joy, however small, alongside a committed effort to cultivate distractions to stop us from focussing on those things which we know will bring us darkness, is the way to leading a happier life. A wise person does not focus on life too closely. Life doesn't bear close scrutiny.**

Chapter One

Symptoms of Mental Disorders

It may be that the first signs have appeared, but not been recognised by you as such, for some time. This illness has often been referred to as 'the curse of the strong.' Having to appear strong, which can be of paramount importance to those of us who are so afraid of showing what we perceive as weakness, can have the negative effect of causing us to delay asking for help until the illness has taken hold and progressed much further than it otherwise would.

Below are just some of the symptoms which might occur – they are warning signs, especially if more than one or two apply, and may be an indication that you need to seek advice:

Fearfulness, particularly at bedtime.

A lack of confidence or low self-esteem (even self-loathing); feeling that you are a bad person as well as a weak one (which can lead to self-harm in some cases).

An inability to sleep over a long period of time – lying awake at night with pervasive worrying or frightening thoughts which you are unable to 'switch off.'

Tearfulness, very brittle emotions, and excessive sensitivity.

Complete lethargy, lack of motivation, lack of enthusiasm for life.

A feeling of helplessness, loss of control and an inability to look forward to the future (even the next day); being convinced that all good experiences are in the past and the future promises none.

Feelings of guilt, weakness or worthlessness (of being one of life's failures).

A sense of injustice, of being a victim.

A perceived need to constantly strive for perfection in yourself (and to expect the same from those around you), together with incessant self-criticism.

Experience of nightmares or hallucinations. (Sleep paralysis, which can be extremely frightening and is a known sleep condition can take on new meaning to someone who may already be vulnerable.)

A sense of isolation from even close family and friends who, you are convinced, would never understand, as you seem powerless to communicate the way you feel, to others.

Anger with yourself and the rest of the world; feeling others are to blame for your situation.

Suicidal thoughts.

If you are experiencing some, or all, of the above and they have continued for more than two or three weeks maximum, the first step is to see your doctor. This takes immense courage and shows **you really are strong**. The old 'pull yourself together, what have **you** got to be worried about?' attitude will not be your doctor's approach and he/she should be able to diagnose any signs of clinical depression. If you do not receive a sympathetic ear then see another doctor. Your doctor may not have a wealth of expertise in treating mental illness and, of course, has limited time to listen personally, but should be able to refer you to a mental health practitioner who **will** be able to help, should the initial medication you may be prescribed not be effective. Try to overcome the nagging doubts which might pervade your mind at this vulnerable time, which are trying to convince you that you will be judged, or quietly ridiculed. Unfortunately, in these current times, your doctor will no doubt have seen many such cases at his surgery.

If your doctor prescribes medication there and then, it is important that you take it exactly as prescribed. If you suffer any negative reactions, go back to your GP right away, there will be other medications you can try. Also, ensure you comply explicitly with the instructions – if you are advised not to drink alcohol, for example, make sure you follow that advice. Some people use alcohol as a way of attempting to blot out everything which is troubling them but, if they are already in a dark place, alcohol will pull them down still further. Alcohol is acknowledged as being a factor in accentuating your mood, whatever that might be.

This initial prescription can be the crutch you need to support you through the most debilitating part of your illness whilst you are preparing to climb the long ladder back up to being yourself once more. Your mental health practitioner may also prescribe tablets to help you to sleep better. Longer and better-quality sleep can, **on its own**, be a **major** factor in your recovery.

If you are advised to take time away from work in order to rest, you must **accept** this. If your first concern is how you will be perceived by employers or work colleagues, be aware that there will be time enough to talk to them later when you will have the opportunity to explain just how ill you have been. In the meantime, try to use a trusted friend or family member as an intermediary for you with regard to work-related issues, sickness certificates, etc. You may be surprised at a later stage to discover just how much empathy exists for your illness from work colleagues who may have endured something similar – either way, resist the compulsion to **imagine** what they may be thinking. This is something you will be able to practise more in learning about **cognitive behavioural therapy** as you gradually recover. If you have **major** work-related problems which have to be addressed during your absence, you will need to talk this through with someone who can advise in this area, **once you are able to think clearly.** But be assured that there is **no alternative** – it is likely that in the long run you will have to address these problems as they may not go away of their own accord, and may be more difficult to resolve the longer this is delayed. A controlled conversation about any issues which may seem insurmountable and the way that you are **feeling** as a result may be the only way forward and will, at least, leave no doubt as to your concerns. Your employer may welcome a frank, open discussion.

Chapter Two

How to help yourself

Remember, you are not mad or bad or weak or abnormal because you are suffering with depression.

I have seen depression described as being anger, directed inwards, towards oneself.

Thinking bad thoughts towards yourself, or others, produces bad feelings.

Whether you are trying to combat depression whilst living on your own or with the support of a loving family or friends, there are things that you can do **practically** to help yourself, both in the short term and in the relatively near future.

Firstly, take the prescribed medication as per Chapter One. Follow the instructions to the letter.

If you are struggling to sleep at night, as much as you will feel like giving in to that sensation, **try not to sleep during the day** - be as active as possible, even if it is only for a short walk outside. It will probably be the last thing you will want to do ('I'm too tired; I don't look attractive; it's rainy or cold; people may want to speak to me' – the excuses will be endless). The truth is, however, that even the smallest amount of activity to begin with, particularly taken outside in the fresh air, will be invaluable as one of the most important and beneficial things you can do as part of your fight back to health. Just being outside benefits both your body and mind. Your rule of thumb should be: **Action first and motivation will quickly follow.**

Gather information from health care professionals – your doctor or your psychiatric nurse if you have been assigned one, with regard to any of your specific worries e.g., panic attacks. Many of us are

aware by now that they arise as a result of our fight or flight response when we feel insecure or threatened and there are strategies which can be used to help us to deal with them.

A panic attack is a severe attack of anxiety and fear which occurs suddenly, often without warning and for no apparent reason. Various other symptoms then occur during a panic attack which can include one or more of the following:

Palpitations or a thumping heart; sweating and trembling; hot flushes or chills; feeling short of breath, sometimes with choking sensations; chest pains; feeling sick, dizzy or faint; fear of dying or going insane; numbness or pins and needles; feelings of unreality, or being detached from yourself.

These symptoms do not mean that there is a physical problem with your heart or chest. They mainly occur because of an overdrive of nervous impulses from the brain to various parts of the body. During a panic attack you tend to over-breathe (hyperventilate) which can cause more symptoms and make the attack even more frightening, thereby amplifying the symptoms again.

An attack will usually last about 5 – 10 minutes, but sometimes they come in waves for up to two hours.

Trying to understand them is in itself helpful, and you can try to deal with them by, for instance, breathing as slowly and as deeply as you can whilst concentrating on your breathing. Breathing into a paper bag helps, by correcting the blood acid level that had been upset by over breathing as by this method you re-breathe in your own carbon dioxide.

Try to be as **disciplined with regard to a daily routine as you possibly can** until your exhausted brain can help you **think** your way back to feeling that you are making an improvement. Try to **eat regularly** and healthily, however little, and to have a **routine for personal hygiene** – nothing will make you feel worse than sitting around for hours on end, unwashed and dishevelled.

Do it for yourself, and no-one else. **Do simple things to give structure to your day** – perhaps watching favourite films, especially those which might be inspirational to you, listening to your favourite music, watching a favourite sport, doing some family research by looking through old photographs or researching the history of the area where you live at present. Looking at pictures of times past (especially those which include photos of previous generations) can help put things into perspective and make us aware of life's challenges generally, rather than viewing them so intensely from a personal perspective. Depression is a form of self-absorption which becomes even more detrimental to our mental health if we add self-loathing.

Contact numbers for trusted people can be reassuring – being able to stay with family or friends at this time offers immense comfort. If this is not possible then have phone numbers at hand for professionals or family/friends whom you **know** you could contact if you are experiencing panic driven thoughts **particularly at night** (including the number for your local Samaritans organisation). A list of helpful contacts and organisations can be found at the back of this book.

Avoid looking at your watch/clock if you wake up at night – the hours will seem endless if you do. Some people find that **listening to a radio** by their bed, quietly in the background, can provide a feeling of being with company and may help you drift off to sleep again. **Audio books** of your favourite authors can help too.

Avoid eating or drinking caffeine after 7 p.m.

Buy yourself a little treat if you are able each day, to help lift your mood. It doesn't have to be expensive; it could be a magazine or something nice to eat, or perhaps some bed linen, some chocolate, a book, some music you love, room perfume or flowers. If you don't feel like going out to do this, perhaps a loved one would do this for you. You don't even need to spend money.

In some cases, just a personal kindness such as someone offering to do their hair for them could be mood enhancing. In other words: anything you can think of that would help to raise self-esteem and lift your mood.

Some things you can practice mentally:

Keep telling yourself to be **gentle on your mind** – think of how you would try to help and support a friend or close family member who might not be feeling themselves and direct this **empathy towards yourself.** Try mentally acting as your own defence barrister and to **use gentleness and patience** with yourself throughout the challenging period of the next few weeks or months.

Keep telling yourself that there is light at the end of the tunnel and that one day you will come through this experience and feel stronger for having done so. You will have learned life skills that you may never have even been aware of in the past, and they may be skills that a lot of others may not possess. This will be **another boost to your self-esteem. You can take these skills forward for the rest of your life and they will be invaluable.**

Make sure you try not to let that inner critic get the better of you. Tell yourself that now is the time to rest and heal – there will be plenty of time, further down the road to recovery, for you to start thinking things through with regard to the future. Try as much as you are able to live for today, and be aware that a lot of things in life, with some obvious exceptions, are the result of choices we have made and can therefore be changed in a lot of cases if there is a will to do so. We can talk about the exceptions-and the obstacles to this, further on in the book.

Do your utmost to try to have patience with your loved ones who may be looking after you as well as they are able. Even though this may be extremely difficult for you in your current state of mind and even **if** you **may**, at this stage, think that they are in some way to blame for what has happened to you or that they are deliberately minimising your symptoms.

When you are feeling better you can talk through any family/friend issues with them which are troubling you but, if they are there for you at present, that is surely a sign of their love for you. Depression is, by its very nature, an inevitably 'selfish' illness as you are focussing **internally** until you start to recover, leaving you unaware of the needs and emotions of others.

Use logic as soon as you are possibly able. Question every anxious thought/belief that you have held to be indisputable or sacred which may have ultimately led to your feeling increasingly more depressed. This may be so deep rooted that you find it hard to question, let alone discard. However, it will be the key to helping your logical brain overcome your negative feelings with regard to your worth, 'deserved' victimisation, the intervention of fate and thereby the negative path for which you are destined.

Try to hang on in there – **things will get better.**

You are NOT what you think, but what you THINK, YOU ARE.

Chapter Three

Helping a loved one survive depression

The first emotions you feel may be those of shock and desolation. You may hardly recognise the person you know and love. Negativity will pervade every fibre of their being – their eyes may appear dull and lifeless, their tone of voice sound expressionless and monotonal; they may appear childlike at times and they may be snappy and critical towards you. Inevitably there will be times when a suggestion you have made, which was well meant, will be regarded by them as a criticism. It might be received as an indication that, from their perspective, you do not know how they are feeling, and so you couldn't possibly understand. As such your suggestions are useless, to say the least. They may, as a result, be abruptly dismissed.

Your loved one may also, if their depression is severe, suddenly switch off and go into a deep sleep during daytime, with their eyes **open**, having previously been holding a conversation with you, which can be very disconcerting to witness for the first time.

Until they return to their more recognisable, former self here are some suggestions as to what **not** to do:

Don't tell them to 'pull themselves together' – they would, if they could.

Don't tell them how lucky they are, compared to so many other people in the world – although they are not thinking logically, they probably already know that and pointing it out will just make them feel even more guilty and weak, if that is possible. Guilt is already ingrained in them for 'allowing themselves' to be in this predicament. There will always be some people who appear to get off lightly in life and others who have more than their fair share of suffering, but it is not always the second group who succumb to depression. It is far more complex than that.

Don't try to use logic to help them at this stage if they are expressing anxiety over something which appears to be easily solvable and trivial to you. They will probably not absorb the suggestion and, even if they did, they would inevitably substitute that worry with another which may seem equally trivial to you. Too much advice in the early stages may fall on deaf ears and it may be difficult to fathom what has brought them to this stage – love and care, listening to them once they want to talk, and encouraging them to communicate their feelings as much as they are able to comprehend them at this stage, will hopefully give immense consolation. Providing meals for them and monitoring their medication are practical things you can do that may help them to realise just how much they are loved and valued.

If the downhill road was started by a sense of injustice **try not to vocally apportion blame** at this stage (particularly towards yourself, if for some reason you feel that way). Do not 'demonise' any person or persons you feel may be responsible – it will just reinforce the overwhelming feeling of victimisation, or even support their conviction, in some cases, that what has happened to them was the hand of fate. Judgemental views (however well intentioned) will not be helpful in the very early stages. There will be time enough later to look more carefully at possible causes which may have led to their illness and what might be needed to resolve the situation, as part of a gradual recovery programme. For now, your loved one is still trying to walk, and will not be able to even think about a marathon, which is probably how they are viewing the thought of coping with the rest of their life.

Try not to be judgmental towards them – accept that their depression is an illness, the same as any other, whilst caring for them until they are able to communicate with you articulately once more. At present they will no doubt be confused and unable to understand what it is that has completely overwhelmed their body and mind.

Don't appear shocked if they voice suicidal thoughts - as harrowing as it may make you feel, it has to be accepted (as gently and quietly on your part as you are able) that this is the way they are feeling, and soft words, quiet listening and expression of your love for them is what they need (not condemnation or any expression of how it is wrong or selfish for them to feel this way). **They** need to make their practitioner aware of their thoughts because, unless they are under age, you will not be able to intervene/speak for them. The diagnosis, progress and conversations between them and the professional who is helping them remain confidential, although you **will** be able to communicate your thoughts to the professional as to how **you** are observing their progress and you can, of course, ask for advice regarding their care.

For yourself, during this painful time, don't try to struggle on if you feel that you are becoming too badly affected by giving your support – sometimes, the person who is very close to the patient is not the best person to help, as they are **too** emotionally attached. You will need resilience and, ideally, some support yourself (even practical help can be invaluable, such as someone helping you with preparation of meals) as well as, perhaps, some respite time to yourself (as you could be needed at any time virtually 24 hours a day at the beginning). Be sure that you **do** think of yourself, as you will be unable to help if you become exhausted and ill.

As far as is possible, whilst trying to retain your own positivity, show empathy – can we imagine how it must feel to be so frightened at the loss of control of your being and thoughts; loss of self-esteem, independence, hope and even identity, whilst struggling to find your way back up the ladder from a very deep pit?

Chapter Four
What causes depression/what type of person might be affected?

Mental health specialists appear to generally agree that **anyone** can be subject to depression:

rich, poor, healthy, unhealthy, young or old, those with good or bad childhood experiences or relationships, those who have had work related problems or successful careers. Even whether one regards oneself as good looking or unattractive to others doesn't necessarily predict a pre-disposition towards mental problems. Scientists have been looking into how much significance can be attributed to a genetic factor with regard to mental sickness. Certainly, there appears to be a possibility that a resilience which is present in some personalities might help some of us to endure life's challenges and misfortunes more stoically than others.

One person may have an ability to cope with relentless pressure, or at least manage their emotions, whilst another may buckle under half the load. There may be major events in someone's life such as the loss of a loved one, a broken relationship, a serious illness or trauma, or seemingly hopeless financial difficulties. The loss of a job, for instance, can trigger a feeling of isolation from work colleagues and even a loss of self-respect, as well as that of income. The list is endless, and whilst some of these traumas will take some people to the lowest depths, others may be able to accept and confront the situation as a challenge, whatever it may be, using the philosophy 'such is life.' Sometimes it is a sense of injustice which will gnaw away at our inner strength until we cannot sleep. That life is not always fair is something which we can find so hard to accept. Depression could arise from persecution by, or a personality clash with, others at our workplace or at home, or by a partner who is manipulative and controlling, resulting in a loss of our inner sense of self-worth.

Where one person will plunge into the depths of despair, another will (even in similar circumstances and perhaps feeling the situation equally deeply) manage to survive emotionally without descending into full blown depression.

When the brain is trying to deal with too much pressure, it has been compared to a dam, trying to hold back an even greater volume of water as river after river becomes flooded. The brain ultimately has to shut down as a defence mechanism for its own self-preservation in order to rest and recover.

I believe that the answer to why we react differently can be due to a number of factors, which depend on different scenarios. Let's not try to diagnose too deeply, at this stage, whether nature or nurture is the dominant factor in sparking the onset of depression at a particular time.

I do firmly believe though that none of us can truly **know** whether we would be prone to succumbing to depression until we are tested. I tend to think of someone sat on the edge of a swimming pool, at the deep end, serenely taking in the warming rays of the sun. Suddenly, with no **apparent** warning, someone comes up behind them and pushes them into the pool. The comparative temperature is cold, producing that first, intense shock when least expecting it and this would be felt by **anyone**, but the person who can, even instinctively, swim or at least scrabble back to safety would probably recover from that shock relatively quickly. Another person, who cannot swim and for whom the shock leaves them helpless and unable to cope, would panic and make chances of survival so much harder. Lifeguards are now telling us to just try to float on our backs if we are in trouble, giving us the chance to think and consider our best options, rather than thrashing about, wasting energy and lessening our chances of survival. The question is: how have we 'learnt to swim' mentally? Could it be partly genetic? Could it have been learned gradually from life's experiences or from wise people who have guided us (perhaps inadvertently) through life? How much is due purely to the physical make up of our brain?

Perhaps life experiences could be compared to being given a vaccination against a particular disease – if we have learnt to cope with adversity gradually and in smaller ways as we grow up, does this give us a certain amount of immunity against buckling under life's challenges in later years?

At some time, we need to acknowledge that life is not always fair and some things have to be accepted. This could be an argument against giving our children a childhood which is too loving, too sheltered or too protected (although we all know and appreciate the opposite philosophy of giving them all the love and nurturing we can to stand them in good stead for dealing with the harsh realities of life.) It is a very fine balance between the two.

As adults, we can learn life skills ('swimming lessons') through Cognitive Behavioural Therapy, but which of us thinks we need to learn any mental skills until, and if, we feel we have a need to (i.e., until we have already been subject to the effects of depression)? The thought will probably never have occurred to us - who feels they **need** to learn to swim if they don't enjoy the experience of being in the water and so don't plan to be swimming anyway? Unless they envisage that it is an invaluable skill, should they ever need to draw on it, it would probably never cross their mind. For some of us, having perhaps led completely sheltered lives, **expectations may be too high,** and when we find ourselves adrift in a storm, we are unable to cope emotionally with the reality of life.

Depression nearly always involves a loss of some kind, and there are so many major losses we can encounter through life. Probably when we think about loss it is the loss of a much-loved lifetime partner or other close family member which initially comes to mind, and how that would be such a shattering experience, signalling the end of a meaningful existence. If we are lucky enough to have close, loving relationships, we could imagine it would seem like an eternity before the painful loss could be accepted in even the smallest way. There might be a period of depression in the meantime, where support is needed to be able to look forward to a different but still meaningful way of life. Some might prefer to keep themselves to themselves, and if this works best for them it should be respected too, without cajoling from well-meaning others.

But In the case of **clinical depression** there may be no **obvious** loss which is apparent to the outsider. This makes it very difficult for others to understand, particularly those who feel that they have endured far worse experiences themselves and may, as a result, be lacking in patience and sympathy.

Some people mourn the loss of their past, their youth, their dreams and ideals, a happy childhood, the growing up of their children whereby they no longer feel needed, their former intelligence and dignity as they age and, therefore, their self-worth. Some mourn what they perceive as a loss of respect, when their working life comes to an end or a lack of justice in a given situation and others, a loss of their dignity, if they need personal care in old age. This is the time, too, when some mourn the loss of their perception of the ordered world they have been a part of during their lifetime: the ease with which they were able to find a post office or a local bank or ask a doctor to make a home visit, or feel safe to be out on the street (life in the 21st century is a challenge to a lot of elderly people, even though they are at the same time reaping the modern benefits of such things as advanced medical knowledge and entertainment in their own home at the press of a button.) There are so many feelings of loss which can be experienced in anyone's lifetime, sometimes subconsciously and, if allowed to develop, by focussing on them intensely, the sadness can be overwhelming.

In Lewis Wolpert's book *Malignant Sadness: The Anatomy of Depression*, he describes depression as being "a sadness which becomes out of control, which grows and grows like a cancer until it can no longer be borne. A sadness which can ultimately consume us until we surrender to it completely and are helpless in its wake."

There are some lines in Alan Bennett's play *Forty Years On*, spoken by a young man who is standing on the rooftop of an English country house, during the First World War, imagining he could hear the guns in France. The lines read:

I would like to think that on that summer night in 1914 the shiver I felt was one of foreboding. But if I shivered, I feel it was only because it was the hour before dawn and cold up there on the roof. And if I felt a shadow come across the moment it was only because young, rich and as I see now, happy, I could afford to feel melancholy.

Some of us can 'afford' melancholy and some of us, cannot, the price is just too high. There are times in our lives when we may be able to afford it and other times when we may not, depending on how emotionally strong we are at that particular time.

Thinking 'Wasn't it all lovely when…' can be a nostalgic trip to happy times past for some of us, giving us golden memories that can never be taken away. If we know, however, that we cannot look back at those times with a warm feeling and then put them back in the box of memories we will be happier not putting ourselves in that vulnerable state in the first place. If we can't let go of them, as we all have to do, without feeling overwhelming sadness at their demise and without viewing the future as a chance to make **more** happy memories, then we are punishing ourselves and surrendering the chance of **making** these new memories by living constantly in the past.

Dwelling on things for some people is not conducive to good mental health. This is what we do when we first move towards the depressive state of mind – we re-run, over and over, what is troubling us (either in the past, or present) and re-live the trauma of events/situations which we have never resolved, or long incessantly for events which have brought us happiness in the past but are no longer there. We reinforce the loss, trauma, anxiety, guilt, or whatever emotion comes to the forefront of our mind as we experience them again in our imagination. It is **never** resolved and, therefore, remains in our subconscious to trouble us, especially at night.

Some kind of distraction/resolution is needed to stop this becoming too intense and an ever-increasing vicious circle.

There are times in life when distraction can become extremely difficult – recovering from illness or injury, for example, or after retirement when the opportunity presents itself to relax and do very little. In the case of retirement, this may be regarded as a very pleasant prospect whilst we are working to provide for our families, but we always need to bear in mind the possible pitfalls of having **too much** time to **think. Too much** time can be as hazardous to good mental health as too little time, when we lead stressful, busy lives. Both have the potential to affect serenity of mind.

Chapter Five

Change

The acclaimed psychiatrist Dorothy Rowe said that she always told her patients that, to get better, they would need to change. She explains in her book *Depression: The Way Out of Your Prison* that the way the patient is **thinking** is what has brought them to this point: "It follows, therefore that if a **way of thinking** has caused the illness, then **a different way of thinking** is what will make the difference to their life. Change of attitude can change a person's life... Change is always frightening because we can never predict exactly what will happen."

She believes that the person inside us who thinks and acts is a fiction: "the self is simply a collection of thoughts, feelings and perceptions. It seems that we need to make some adjustment to them if we are to lead a happier life." She wrote that "good people are those people who feel that they are never good enough."

One theory is that the period during which one is recovering from depression can be likened to a darkroom, where you have the opportunity to **develop** the image of the next chapter in your life. Making a concerted effort to **think** in a different way requires immense courage and determination. Some people do not want to give up their thought identity (i.e. their perceived self) which they cling to, as the alternative seems uncertain and frightening to them. After all, this 'self', as they perceive it, has been their identity over however many years.

Pulling up anchor on what we have known as 'I' for a very long time, can be extremely daunting. This has been their persona until now and setting sail in uncharted waters can make them feel adrift in the world, with no maps and no guide to show the way. Even if they **are** able to acknowledge that this way of thinking has helped lead them towards emotional distress, they **may** proudly feel that it is what makes them different, individual, less naïve than others perhaps, and therefore more **realistic** about the negative side of life.

In some cases, they may feel that this means they are more intelligent than others. There may even be a negative arrogance which has developed over time and may call for some humility.

Depression can be the best teacher of humility. Making the first steps to giving up your 'self' and being willing to consider how you may have **perceived** life's challenges, the way you have **reacted** to them, and how this may all have affected your mental health, is the beginning of a newer, more positive outlook. It can make all the difference. Cognitive Behavioural Therapy, which I will mention in more detail further on in this book, teaches us a way of challenging each potentially harmful perception by giving an opportunity to view it in an alternative way, before it lodges in our subconscious.

Practised humility can result in us becoming confident to accept our lack of ability in those things in life which we are not good at, to the extent that even if others find that amusing, we are able to laugh **with** them. Those who have this attribute are often the most popular individuals in society.

Dorothy Rowe explains that our self is constantly telling itself a story about itself. "Our memories tell us about our past and thus define who we are now and what we shall become. Most importantly, our memories need to fit in with our aims to be acceptable to ourselves and others and to feel secure. The things we can't forget are memories which do not fit into our aims."

She adds that personal pride prevents us from resolving some issues which haven't gone according to our ideas. Apart from perhaps feeling despair and anguish we may "feel our 'self' shattering and falling apart, If the ideas we have of our self are not an accurate presentation. Every time your memory of an event comes into your mind, it is demanding that you work on the business of constructing new ideas. We can't bear that other people see us as a failure, or accept that the world is a dangerous place… When certain memories haunt us we need to ask ourselves, what is it in this memory that offends my pride? And when we find the answer and accept it, we can let the memory go."

I couldn't recommend Dorothy Rowe's books to you highly enough. She teaches that "What determines our behaviour is not what happens to us, but how we interpret what happens to us… Interpretation is something we create, and we're free to change it." She tells us that "what is called madness is really immense mental distress and an inability to cope." Her philosophy is that "you're lucky or unlucky, that's it. When people begin to accept that, they no longer need therapy. Happiness is not a goal but a by-product of accepting and valuing yourself."

The key to a happy life is our state of mind – how we view the world and what skills we possess in order to tolerate others by observing them from other than a purely subjective point of view. An intolerance of others to the point where it can lead us to feel stressed and angry ultimately leaves us open to depression. We cannot **control** the character of **others** and harbouring hateful thoughts can be detrimental to our **own** physical and mental health as the **anger** and frustration turns **inward on ourselves.** But what if we have **tried** to voice our feelings, to resolve issues in order to avoid keeping them inside and **no-one listens** or, at least, appears to do the 'fair/just' thing, as we see it? This may then add victimisation to our already full to overflowing pot of harmful emotions.

Life **is** unfair, there are so many issues about which we may feel passionate, so many issues we would like to have the power to be able to control. But if we **concentrate and focus on the dark side of life**, constantly sitting in the shadows, the darkness will eventually consume us. This doesn't mean we have to give up and say there is no point. We need, instead, to focus on the **solution** and the contribution, however small, we can make in working to achieve that goal.

Changes in world affairs, for example, sometimes appear to happen suddenly, whereas it is more often than not the culmination of years of determination on the part of those individuals who have been seeking that change with passion and commitment. It doesn't even always happen in their lifetime but they are relentless in their pursuit of the change they desire.

Focus on the solution, rather than the problem. This is the mentally healthy way forward. Start with very small steps and remember you will be unable to help yourself or others if you allow your negativity to pull you into a state of depression and inactivity. There are likely to be charities working for a cause about which you feel strongly, too, and you may be able to contribute in whatever way you are able to support them. You may be able to help with their fundraising, by signing a petition or even just by spreading the word. No doubt you will then be able to see how major changes can occur with persistence and determination.

We have a choice - we don't have to be naïve enough to believe that life is perfect; we merely need to refuse to let it deplete us of any enthusiasm for life, robbing us of energy to face a new day **which always has the potential to motivate and bring us joy as well as to discourage us**.

How can we begin to try to change personally? / What aspects of our personality may be harmful to good mental health?

Learning to control our anger is of paramount importance in achieving a good state of mind. It is not bad or wrong to feel angry: often it is the trigger for us to do something constructive about a situation which we find no longer tolerable, whether it is a personal problem or even a global crisis. If we feel we can no longer **accept** it we need to find a way to do something constructive about it - just **thinking** about it and turning it over and over in our mind makes our **anger turn inward, on ourselves**. **Anger is a force** which we need to be able to **control** in order to survive mentally. That's what makes the difference. We **can** learn to do this, by recognising the trigger points which light our anger fuse and the subsequent physical signs we feel **before** we erupt.

We can then, with practice, learn methods by which to calm ourselves in order to behave in a rational fashion rather than losing control.

One can easily imagine the intense anger which would need to be controlled by, for instance, an NSPCC or RSPCA inspector. If resolution of the problem seems unattainable, talk to a trusted, loving friend or family member and ask for help. Don't keep it to yourself. However big the problem, you will start to find the answer if you ask for help, perhaps even by speaking to a professional, a charity worker or a counsellor. Concentrate on the change you want to see, **visualise it** and start working towards it with your first, small steps.

What kind of personality would you like to 'try on?' Try to make an honest list of how you would describe yourself to an imaginary, trusted confidante. Not just how you look, but your personality, views and inner thoughts as well as your relationships and communication with others. Now go through the list and highlight in one colour the points you feel proud of and, with another colour, the points you would like to change in order to make your life easier (and perhaps more compatible with others). You will find there will not be many that are impossible to change if you are truly committed.

If you feel you would like to be considered as a kind person, for example, yet do not consider you have it within you, why not try **acting** in a kind way and see how it feels? It is not hypocritical if it is something that you genuinely would like to work towards becoming - the recipient of your kindness would still benefit from your caring act. As long as this is done without any intention to manipulate or control the other person, nor to expect something in return, the experience may present you with a new feeling of increased self-esteem and a different outlook on life, with motivation to believe in the change you wish to see in yourself. There are not likely to be many characteristics that are not open to change, if we practice determinedly enough. They may ultimately become part of the past as our new personality becomes second nature.

You might like to make another list of what you-would choose to aspire to be. Some wishes, being taller for instance, may be impossible to achieve. But you may be surprised at what is possible with a will to change into a personality that allows you to feel at ease with yourself instead of constant inner conflict between your inner and outer 'you' and your relationship with others. Being happy with who you are is a precious thing in life. You don't have to achieve the same as, or think in the same way as others to avoid being ridiculed. Try openly and without apologies to express your differences in a conversation. If this is done confidently and perhaps even with humour, the majority of people will respect you and even like you for it. They should certainly be aware that they cannot make you feel inferior. "No one can make you feel inferior without **your** consent." (Eleanor Roosevelt)

Chapter Six

The learning process – the climb back up

American author Tom Robbins writes that "all depression has its roots in self-pity and all self-pity is rooted in people taking themselves too seriously".
Perhaps the climb up, the need to start again, could be viewed as **a pity, but that is all.**

The **smallest step** up from the bottom of the pit to the summit brings hope. Hope is a motivator which will have seemed, perhaps for a long time to have vanished from your life.

Recognising every negative thought and questioning it, as you become stronger, helps you to stop thinking that you will never get better. You will find it harder and it will take longer to recover if you insist that you are never going to feel better, that no one will ever understand you and that you will never be yourself again.

The day will come though when you will **know** that you have turned the corner. It may be just a small change in outlook initially, a better night's sleep, or a conscious enjoyment of something like a meal, a conversation or a walk.

It may not be a continuous climb – there may be delays, days with setbacks, but the **improvement** will be **felt** as such by you and by those who have helped you come this far. A brightness in the eyes that was lacking before, less heaviness in the tone of voice, or perhaps an interest, however small, in people or places around you, will be evident.

You may feel like a child having to learn to walk again but, nevertheless, you **have** walked before and **will do again**. These first, stumbling steps are everything – they form the basis of what will be a re-entry into the 'race of life' – certainly not a sprint to begin with, but a slow and sure start to the marathon of the rest of your life. A marathon at a safe and measured pace, with a more astute awareness of the pitfalls which can affect your mental health. A marathon in which living your everyday life may require valuable pit stops so that choices can be wisely considered and negativity can be recognised as such when making decisions.

You will have recovered from a state of virtual 'non-existence' to a chance for a new start in life, putting the past behind you, together with any feelings that were destructive and counter-productive in helping you to become the new person you **choose** to be. You will have developed new tools to help you with your new lifestyle. Picture yourself as feeling mentally in control and calm, and think of it as the ultimate last word to anyone whom you would have once **considered,** rightly or wrongly, as someone who wished you ill, and whose opinion is no longer of major importance to you anyway.

This climb will eventually progress, right to the top if you persistently endeavour to put effort into your recovery and to LEARN.

Learning is the key to managing your mental health for the future. Put into practice the new life and social skills you have learnt – you will find them invaluable. (A guide to them, with the examples as to how Cognitive Behavioural Therapy can help you is explained later in this chapter, albeit briefly.)

You may have learnt to swim but, depending on the severity of stormy waters which may lie ahead, you will at least be able to recognise what is in effect an SOS call to yourself **at a much earlier stage**. If you **do** feel that you need some help and support, you will be more confident in asking for this, without shame, **before** the illness has had a chance to take hold to the same extent. Your learning will have helped you to realise that your previous feelings of guilt and failure are just the **symptoms of your illness and not the cause.**

There are many excellent books which can help you to lead a full, mentally balanced life once more.

Cognitive Behavioural Therapy has helped very many people in situations with which you may be able to identify and David D Burns's book *Feeling Good – The New Mood Therapy* is one such. It may seem quite daunting to some, especially at first, when you are struggling to concentrate but taken slowly, perhaps two or three pages at a time, it is of immense help. If nothing else, it makes one aware of the way in which a mode of thinking can lead to a particular state of mind. It states that "feelings aren't facts" and describes the danger of jumping to conclusions. It reinforces the idea that arbitrarily jumping to a negative conclusion may not be justified by the facts – this kind of unhelpful way of thinking is labelled as **'mind reading'** or **'the fortune teller error**.' It helps to make you aware of how your brain **can** interpret everyday experiences in a negative way, resulting in destructive thoughts and actions, or lack of action. It gives us examples of 'fortune telling', leading to the conviction that something bad is going to happen, or that someone hates us or regards us as worthless. We interpret a certain look, a half-heard conversation or an occasion when a friend fails to meet up with us, for example, in such a way that leaves **no doubt in our mind** that we are not liked or respected by others. In another example, we may be adamant that because we have **failed,** in our eyes, at one thing, we **are a failure in life**, as a whole.

Reading David Burns's book, perhaps with a trusted person, can be doubly helpful as it gives you a chance to highlight any particular sentence, paragraph or chapter which has particularly resonated in your mind. You may then choose to go back to it in more detail because you can personally identify with the feelings raised and would like to talk about it more at a time chosen by you.

CBT helps us to look at things from a different perspective and can open our eyes to the extent that we can, at least, **doubt** whether we know for sure what someone else is thinking at any particular time, or how a particular event is going to pan out.

It can give us confidence (or, at least, the appearance of confidence to begin with) to ask another person whether we have misinterpreted a situation and whether they feel that there is a problem between us. If they reply in the affirmative, then we can at least talk about the situation and try to come to a resolution or a compromise. Others are not always aware of our feelings unless we make it clear to them that something has upset us and **why** it has. There may be times when the help of a professional is needed as a counsellor or mediator but the problem will, as a result, have been brought out into the open and, as such, will not be magnifying internally with no outlet. In many cases, we may discover that we have exaggerated the situation out of all proportion. Alongside this, if we want to enjoy a better quality of life, we **will** have to learn how to accept situations we can't change. Life is full of responsibilities and events that we may not have foreseen, but **the responsibility for our own mental health is, ultimately, our own** and if we have already suffered a period of depression, it should be evident that we need to change our thought pattern.

Even if, for example, you find that work that has no special meaning for you, if you are doing it to provide for you and your family, that in itself is meaningful. The teachings of CBT show us that we can easily construct an idea about ourselves and mistake that for a fact. We can come to learn that the feedback we give ourselves, about ourselves, can be edited as we learn to change into the person we wish to be.

Think, for a moment, about those things in life that we **cannot change**, both in the world around us and on a more personal level, **and those that we can**. The list of those we cannot (albeit some of the hardest we may have to face, such as bereavement) will ultimately need acceptance of a kind with a dedication to finding another purpose in life, if at all possible.

There is **nothing** we can do to stop such changes; all we can do is to try to find some kind of strength within ourselves and with the help and support of loved ones or even counsellors. We may need to make some life changes in order to be able to face our disbelief and sense of overwhelming loss. The fact is, though, that the list of things we **cannot** change is much shorter than those that we **can**, if we so choose. They may not be easy to change, they might require major decisions to change them, there may be priorities to consider, but if the will is there, they are not necessarily **impossible** to change.

Think of all the things we **are** able to change in today's society, which were once not possible. It may seem futile, for example, to try to persuade a teenage girl that looks are transient and that beauty comes from inside, or that it is in the eye of the beholder. The idea that happiness is not dependent on looks may be inconceivable to them, but if we **are** discontented with our looks when we are adult, there are a myriad of professionals in the field of weight loss, cosmetic surgery or hair restoral (just to mention a few). If the problem is of a sexual nature, we can access help from a professional or even buy products from the shelf. If we are unable to conceive naturally, there is treatment available such as IVF or, in the case of same sex couples, the possibility of having children of our own without necessitating the adoption or fostering process. Not every scenario has a happy ending of course, and some treatments may be inadvisable, or unethical, but there is no complete road block as there would have been in the past.

Not all of these changes are–guaranteed to provide lasting happiness, as we have already been learning, but at least the options are there.

Watch out for and try to develop a mental defence against bullying

Bullying, either at school, in the workplace, or on social media seems omnipresent in this day and age. A **change** in how our inner critic views our own personality and assesses how we appear to others **is** achievable, as daunting as it seems. We need to be able to raise our self-esteem in order to be resilient. A young person in school, for instance, who may already be suffering with low self-esteem, will be vulnerable, and will have that already negative view of themselves reinforced, if they are subjected to relentless bullying each day. A skilled professional can help immensely in teaching the best way to react to this sad experience and all schools will now have an anti-bullying policy. The headteacher needs to be alerted in order to allow the situation to be dealt with promptly and most schools now will have a member of staff who is trained in pastoral care as well as a special educational needs co-ordinator.

Both should be able to support the pupil in learning how to improve his/her self-esteem, teaching resilience, offering one-to-one listening support and, if their work has been affected, some quality one-to-one teaching time. Helping to raise someone's self-esteem will give them more confidence, whether to be able to give an answer in class without the fear of making a mistake (which they feel certain will result in a derogatory remark from another pupil who is trying to intimidate them), or to ask a question about something which they might not understand. Confidence can often negate the impact of bullying and is an effective tool in lessening the chances of it occurring again and again as we go through childhood and into adult life.

Be in no doubt, though, that bullying should not be ignored or go unpunished – we do not need to suffer bullying in silence and accept this as normal. A bully should be reprimanded and dealt with accordingly in any situation and at whatever age, whether it happens in the workplace, at school, at home or anywhere else. Bullying is often the cause of suicides amongst young people and it can be of a physical or mental nature.

We need to be sure to look for the signs if we see a change in our loved ones and to make ourselves aware of how bullying is usually defined. Bullying is usually defined as behaviour that is:

- repeated
- intended to hurt someone either physically or emotionally
- often aimed at certain groups, for example because of race, religion, gender or sexual orientation.

  It takes many forms and can include:

- physical assault
- teasing

- making threats

- name calling

- cyberbullying - bullying via mobile phone or online (for example email, social networks and instant messenger)

- encouraging others to ignore or be unresponsive to someone

Your school should have its own policy to stop bullying, as should your workplace.

Helping to raise someone's self-esteem often goes hand in hand with anger management, as pent-up anger often accompanies the feeling of helplessness, and eventually these emotions finally reach boiling point.

One young person confided in me that they wished they were funny because 'everyone loves people who make them laugh.' This is particularly effective if you can make them laugh at your own expense. I'm sure that many of us would love to be an extrovert who could walk into a room and enhance it instantly with our humour and wit.

But, it's no good fretting – if we are not funny, faking it would be apparent, so we might as well just concentrate on other attributes which we will most certainly possess and try to be ourselves. Remember that, just because someone tends to gather a crowd around them, it does not necessarily mean that they are a wonderful person who will always have more friends than yourself. After all, one good friend may be all we need in life. A wealth of knowledge, which can be acquired by an inquisitive, lively mind can be very entertaining too (if not forced on others, at every opportunity) as an alternative to being the life and soul of the party.

Try to learn more about a handful of favourite subjects, as a start, or even topical, non-controversial items in the news which aren't distressing, and there will probably be an opportunity to bring one of them into a conversation appropriate to your 'audience.' Once the ice has been broken you will probably find you will start to relax as your confidence grows, whereby the rest of the conversation may flow more naturally.

Also, showing a genuine interest in the other person and being a good listener is always a likeable attribute.

Be aware, too, that every time you put someone you admire on a pedestal, you diminish your own self value/worth accordingly. Start from the premise that people are going to like you, rather than the negative approach that you will never fit in. They certainly **won't all like you, and you,** equally, will most surely **not like all of them.** What, ultimately, does that matter as long as we just try to be courteous to one another? **Be kind to yourself.**

Chapter Seven

The View from the Summit

Alongside a feeling of unimaginable relief, there may still occasionally be underlying persistent thoughts and questions: How could I have allowed myself to become so ill? What will people think of me when I return to normal day to day situations? Will I ever be as poorly as that again?

The first two questions will have hopefully been answered as part of your thought processes whilst learning the life skills to take you forward in your life. They will have been an integral part of your recovery and your preparation for the future. The last question is probably the one which will fill you with fear and dread. There are two rays of hope, though, to give you comfort when you are feeling this way.

Firstly, nothing in this world had prepared you for the traumatic, life-sapping state of clinical depression the first time you encountered it. **You didn't see it coming**! You have clawed your way back up from that situation once and so that black hole will never have that same impact – you now know that it is not inescapable. You have beaten it once and so you know that you could do it again. Remember that expression 'what doesn't kill you makes you stronger'. Look on it, in medical terms, as being given a vaccination that helps your body to fight any future challenge, should it reoccur.

Secondly, and most importantly, you will have learned so much from your experience and your fight to recover. You know that you are far from being a weak person or a failure, you have proved to yourself that you are a winner, a survivor.

You have the tools now to see it coming, well before it reaches the intensity of the first experience. The learning you have acquired about yourself and your dealings with others, will have also left you much better equipped to recognise negative thoughts and turn them around, before they enter your subconscious.

Start 're-grouping' and rethinking. Always be on the lookout for sources of inspiration – books, films, poetry, music, life stories of inspirational people, songs, quotations. There are some blank pages at the end of this book for you to record your own examples, so that you have made it your personal reference book. You will have made a contribution to the content of 'your' book. You could, alternatively, create your own separate notebook of thoughts of inspiration and hope.

For instance, how did Simon Weston recover from the trauma of his experiences during the Falklands War? How did Christopher Reeve adjust mentally from being Superman to someone who was majorly disabled? There are many such people who can lead by example – Stephen Hawking, for instance, who **continued his work** in the field of astrophysics, adding to the bank of knowledge he left us, against such personal adversity. How is it that some can bring humour into the darkest situations? We are not all born the same but we can try to emulate their coping mechanisms as far as we are able. Some of them might work for us, too.

Conversely, when your mind is fragile, avoid negativity in whatever capacity you encounter it unless you are absolutely positive that it will have no ill effect on you. Whether you might be choosing to watch a film, read a book, mix with friends who are feeling the same helplessness, or whatever you choose to do which you feel suits your own present mood at a given time, the hopelessness will be intensified.

You may not feel that you can be light-hearted but try to resist wallowing in your misery. We are more aware, generally, about which foods may have a harmful effect on our physical body. Equally, if you are not mentally strong enough, you will do far better without a diet of black thoughts, however instinctively their intake might appeal to you. I found the lyrics of a song by George Harrison to be very thought provoking. 'Beware of Darkness' expresses the importance of **awareness** for good mental health and how it can help prevent dark thoughts and influences creeping up on us.

Be mindful, too, of an excessive intake of anything which might lower your mood. Some will always consider alcohol to be helpful when they are stressed and would not want to be persuaded otherwise. Is it wise to drink alcohol excessively when you are already feeling miserable and vulnerable? Its effect, even if you feel that it is helpful, can only ever be temporary and can lead you into other problems. You may have initially thought to use it as a temporary crutch but it can easily become a consistent habit rather than an occasional pleasure. One could ask whether it is sensible to put oneself in a position where you may ultimately not be responsible for your actions and may possibly have to face more serious consequences when you eventually sober up.

If you can sense that there is something, still, in your subconscious mind which needs resolution before your recovery can be complete then **talk** to someone, instead of trying to deal with it yourself, when it is becoming clear that it will not go away. It needs to be someone you can trust and, if it is a mental health professional, remember that you still have a choice. If you feel strongly that delving into your past, like opening a 'Pandora's box' of harmful memories, will not be helpful and just the thought of it is something that horrifies you, then make that clear. No two people are alike and what works for some is not always best for others. It may be that supportive conversations, where you just need someone to listen, will be the way forward, but the choice is yours and no-one is going to force you into doing something that you don't feel happy with. Some people prefer to bury something which they find too painful to discuss.

They may be helped instead, to generally maintain a look forward mentality and to start afresh, managing those painful past experiences and recognising them for what they are (**in the past**) rather than constantly reverting to them in the present, without accepting they are not relevant **to the future**.

What if we find it almost impossible to stop focussing on the situation which we feel got us into the predicament we faced in the first place?

How can we manage the anger we feel towards the person, or people, we consider responsible? It's completely natural to want to blame someone or something for our predicament and it may be that we feel adamant that we are a victim, but the final word lies with us and what happens next in our life is far from inevitable. Our life is not being controlled - what happens next is our own choice and therefore not ordained. We've already learned that anger is one of the most destructive forces we can inflict upon ourselves and so we need to consider our actions/reactions to what has happened very carefully. Considering our choices and, as a result, the consequences is one of the wisest lessons we will learn. If we feel that we have been let down by someone or a particular situation, thinking of the options we have and talking them over with someone who is supportive is a start. There may not be a magic solution but weighing up all aspects of what is important to us (and the family, if applicable) is a good way forward. It may require a considerable compromise to acquire the prize of inner peace – perhaps a calmer, less stressful life may necessitate less income, but it could be the difference between mayhem and serenity. Income, although important if we are to balance the books, is obviously only one aspect of life, but sitting down and discussing how we and our loved ones wish to continue our way of life and what that will require may produce more surprises than we would have thought by way of likeminded priorities.

There may have to be compromises - some challenges are major and involve decisions as to how we will be able to keep a roof over our heads - but others, that we may not have thought of, could be more manageable.

Looking at our expenditure, for instance, and seeing where corners could be cut: could we downsize to a less expensive home, or save money by cooking more meals at home, rather than takeaways or eating out? Could we save money on expensive holidays or mobile phones or running an expensive car, or two cars? If family relationships are strong enough, it may be that where there's a will there's a way, and it's a question of agreeing on priorities.

Of course, for some, it is a constant **struggle** to just **survive** financially, but it is still worth doing the exercise to determine whether lifestyle choices could possibly be re-thought if it means that life is more manageable with more time for family life. Try to frame any decision with 'will it bring me happiness?' Try to think about what you want from life. If you conclude that you have been, and still are, helpless in being able to make the right choices in your life, you may be helped by some professional advice, such as a life coach, your doctor, or (in Britain) your local councillor or MP. There may be income from the government to which you are entitled and have never realised. Seek all the help that you can.

Try to eliminate the word 'should' from your vocabulary. It is at best unhelpful and at worst can make the pressure unbearable. Think instead in terms of 'wouldn't it be nice, if I could' or 'perhaps I could try to...' Doing what feels right for you needs to be a consideration, alongside your unequivocal commitments. Talk it over with loved ones concerned in a quiet, honest way, hopefully helping them to understand, alongside focussed listening to **their** feelings and possible anxieties. The inevitable selfish nature of your illness has probably made you blind to what they have been feeling inside, whilst trying to comprehend what has happened to make their loved one apparently change so much. Is there a new path to walk in life which would be acceptable to all?

If you know you are a perfectionist, try to remember that you **will** make mistakes all through life, as will others – you are only human and, therefore, not perfect. Forgive yourself.

There is usually something very endearing about an individual who has made mistakes but has accepted them, however bad, and subsequently made a positive resolution to learn from them and put them right wherever possible. Remember, too, that you won't be able to help yourself, or others, unless you are prepared to fail sometimes. Consider surgeons, lifeguards and firemen, to name but a few, and how they have to accept that sometimes even their best efforts fall short of saving someone's life. Athletes, too, have to summon up the mental strength to get up and try again, accepting that this time the elusive prize has slipped from their grasp.

Nor do you **always** need to feel that you are right. You **may** be, more often than not, but being right does not always equate to happiness – they are not necessarily the same thing. If you had to choose between the two, which would you choose? This is just some food for thought, but no-one is right **all** of the time and yet some people will turn their backs on happiness, just for the sake of **knowing,** without a shadow of a doubt, that they are right.

Try to find a purpose and a structure to life, however minor you consider it to be, at first. The philosophy of the Dalai Lama teaches that this is our purpose in life - to seek happiness. Happiness, that is, as opposed to instant pleasure. There is a difference. The latter is transient and often has unpleasant consequences. The former is something to work towards, trying to mould our lives with patience and wisdom.

Not an easy state to achieve, but a very precious one. Some may consider that seeking happiness is self-centred and egotistical but 'happy' people are often much more selfless and are inspirational. When one is so miserable it is hard not to be self-focussed and selfish, thereby, other people's needs, even those we really love, can go un-noticed.

Try **acting** out a personality that exudes happiness, **just for a day** to begin with - see how it feels.

Sometimes, a disguised outward appearance of confidence can help you to feel more positive internally.

It doesn't mean you have to try, long term, to be a person you are not. It is merely to allow you to experience, perhaps just for a day, a new 'happy' personality. Try a test run – see how it fits and how it makes you feel.

Chapter Eight

Back Down to Earth

Time, now, to **go forward,** now that you can at least **envisage a future.**

You're moving on, **putting the past behind you**, making its memory less intense (and therefore less painful) and accepting that you have **learnt from this experience. It is not going to ruin and rule the rest of your life.**

Practice vigilance in resisting the temptation to wear your recent period of depression like a badge. Avoid self-labelling – there is always a strong likelihood that it will develop into self-prophecy. You may feel that to have been diagnosed with bipolar disorder, as just one example, puts you in elite company, amongst individuals whom you ardently admire (both past and present) and that, subsequently, the suffering endured as a consequence is worth the price. Supreme intelligence, even genius, in whatever sphere of human achievement, is not exclusive to those who have been afflicted in this way. You could try to make an unprejudiced list of those high achievers who have generally lived in a healthy state of mind, if you are still in doubt. This will be hard to do because we are always quick to believe our own prejudices.

It may be instructive to consider the example of Vincent Van Gogh. Nienke Bakker was curator of an exhibition of his paintings at the Van Gogh Museum. She wrote an article for *The Times* in 2016 entitled 'Alcohol, bipolar disorder, syphilis – the Madness of Vincent Van Gogh' an excerpt from which reads as follows: "In spite of all Van Gogh's illnesses, one of the main messages of the exhibition is that Van Gogh wasn't the crazed visionary whose work was fuelled by the fire of his madness – as he was depicted after his death." In fact, she said, his most brilliant paintings were created in spite of his illness. "When he was really ill, he couldn't paint. He couldn't work, he couldn't even write. So the paintings that are here and the drawings, they were all done in the episodes between episodes."

In the accompanying catalogue to the exhibition Laura Prins writes that "his technique was too considered to have been the result of illness."

How often have we heard the expression 'beautiful and damned' in relation to someone who we think had such potential to be a star, in whatever field, but has died young? The examples are too numerous to mention, but I find myself wondering just how many of these 'beautiful people' could have been successfully treated, if mental health had been the issue, with today's enlightened treatments and medication. Maybe Elvis Presley would have made it to Britain for a countrywide tour, or Virginia Woolf would have delighted her readers with more of her novels.

Try to have a focus and a structure to each day and, as much as possible, allow for some free time, however limited. Notice the simple things around you – look up at the clouds, the stars and the moon. Listen to the song of the blackbird in the summer months and if you're lucky enough to be near the sea, the countryside, or even just a green space, try to really observe the things around you.

After the devastation of the Second World War, amongst the rubble of a bombed building, a close family member observed that there was new growth in the form of a small red campion - the contrast between this little, perfect flower and the mayhem around it giving a sense of euphoria on contemplation of its incredible survival, against all the odds.

We are often told that, had we received a diagnosis of terminal illness, we would start to appreciate the natural things in life which may have gone un-noticed until now. What a shame that it takes such sad news for some people to start experiencing that pleasure. Listening to a beautiful piece of music, watching waves or gazing up at stars gives us a sense of perspective and timelessness and can help take us out of ourselves, enabling us to understand the small length of time we are here on earth. If the concentration was there, who could fail to be emotionally stimulated by the sound of the ocean and the vista of clouds in a blue sky? The tiniest bird sensing the signs of an approaching storm, wastes no time quaking with anxiety, but sets about finding shelter and perseveres until the storm has passed.

If we are oblivious to the world around us, we don't experience the here and now, even if it **is** a beautiful summer's day. An idealistic approach, you might feel, but one which we can try to consciously cultivate whenever an opportunity presents itself. The animal kingdom is primed to use all of its senses and there was a time when man needed to do likewise. Evolution has made us less dependent on them but when we focus on using each and every one that is appropriate to our surroundings it may be a new and rewarding experience to us, whilst at the same time, eliminating that constant **internal,** negative conversation.

The novelist Marcel Proust in his book *In Search of Lost Time* talks about the many projects in which we could find enjoyment and yet our lives allow them to become invisible because we have become lazy, feeling sure of a future and therefore delaying them incessantly. He brings it home to us by writing: "But let all this threaten to become impossible forever, how beautiful it would become again! The cataclysm doesn't happen, we don't do any of it, because we find ourselves back in the heart of normal life, where negligence deadens desire. And yet we shouldn't have needed the cataclysm to love life today. It would have been enough to think that we are humans, and that death may come this evening."

Chapter Nine

Inspiration

The reading of inspirational books, or even just quotations, can help us to keep stress out of our lives. Setting aside even ten minutes each day to read in this way can help to provoke positive thoughts and teach us about wisdom.

At the risk of appearing self-indulgent, I have listed some of my favourites below – hopefully, to encourage you to collect those of your own. Be vigilant in noticing any examples you find which give you, personally, food for thought and seem to reach out and invite you to follow a new philosophy on life or a new pathway to explore.

In *The Wisdom of Donkeys – Finding Tranquillity in a Chaotic World*, Andy Merrifield writes of "Primal

Therapy involving the dismantling of the causes of tension, defence systems and neurosis." Thus "tension is the central motivant of neurotic behaviour, of an inability to switch off, to quieten down, to feel a daydream or to just be." He notes that wisdom is a pathway to warding off the onset of depression.

Seneca, On the Shortness of Life:

"The greatest obstacle to living is expectancy, which hangs upon tomorrow and loses today. You are arranging what is in Fortune's control and abandoning what lies in yours."

For some people old age overtakes them while they are still mentally childish and so they face it unprepared and unarmed. They've not thought ahead at all and have therefore not made any provision for it, stumbling upon it unawares and not realising that it was approaching day by day. In our busy daily lives, we can become so preoccupied that we become aware of just how precious life is, only when it is over.

A state of happiness is something to be striven for and valued. It invariably requires genuine thought and a sense of deep emotion, even some planning (as far as anything in life can be planned) until you really feel that life is good and you can't help but smile.

Sidney Poitier, the accomplished actor, wrote in his book about the philosophy of making love, work and family our foremost considerations in life. He expressed the view that they are the "legacy we leave behind when our little moment in the sun is gone." He wrote that "for most of human history, people were only slightly above the starvation level (in many countries most people still are). Everyone needed to pull together or the whole family wouldn't make it... People found comfort in their commitments and weren't infected by the pleasure principle." He said that avoiding confrontation is not a sign of weakness and that constructive, honest discussions on differences of opinions and a willingness to listen to others is an alternative way forward. Confrontation rarely, he opined, has a positive solution. Sometimes, If compromise is not possible, we have no alternative but to walk away but it's worth considering that you can be right, or you can have a good outcome – it's not necessarily the same thing.

Try to keep a sense of purpose in your life. The philosopher **Colin Wilson** opined that "when human beings are in rebellion, they are rebelling against a breakdown in the value system that had previously sustained them... with the scientific revolution, man came to comprehend that his destiny was in his own hands. Rather than accept the challenge, they have settled for the pseudo comfort of indolence. And the inevitable result of that negative decision has been the emergence of an overwhelming sense of boredom. Humanity is in a malaise that is the direct result of a lack of purpose. We need a sense of purpose."

Fear knocked at the door – Faith answered, and there was no one there. **Proverb**

This, too, shall pass. **The Bible**

Play the hand you're dealt. **Jawaharlal Nehru**

What you focus on, magnifies! **anon**

Life is random and bad things happen to good people. It's unreasonable to single myself out and ask 'Why me?' Look at 9/11 and the 3000 killed by terrorists. Why them? **Christopher Reeve, 'Still Me'**

Never be a prisoner of your past. It was just a lesson, not a life sentence. **anon**

Unborn tomorrow and dead yesterday – why fret about them if today be sweet? I have since been told that hallucinations and dreams and insomnia are normal symptoms of over fatigue and excessive strain and that, had I consulted an intelligent doctor……I might have been spared the exhausting battle against nervous breakdown. **Vera Brittain, 'Testament of Youth'**

Truly, for some men nothing is written unless THEY write it. **from the film 'Lawrence of Arabia'**

The best time to plant a tree was 20 years ago. The second best time is to plant it now. **Old Chinese proverb**

Carpe Diem – Seize the Day **Horace**

Never, never, never give up. **Winston Churchill**

Nothing in life is permanent – not even one's troubles.
Charlie Chaplin

Courage is being scared to death, but saddling up anyway.   **John Wayne**

Fear can't hurt you, any more than a dream.   **Sir William Golding**

Happiness is an inside job. **William Arthur Ward**

Honesty is the first chapter in the book of wisdom.
Thomas Jefferson

Each believes easily, what he fears and what he desires.
La Fonteine

We are such stuff as dreams are made on and our little life is rounded with a sleep. **William Shakespeare**

Is all that we see and seem but a dream within a dream? **Edgar Allan Poe**

I don't get stressed, I gave that up about 15 years ago, but only experience pushes stress away. **Ridley Scott**

If you can meet with triumph and disaster and treat those two imposters just the same... **Rudyard Kipling, 'If'**

This last quotation is inscribed over the doorway on to the courts at Wimbledon tennis courts. I always wonder whether it has particular significance for John McEnroe, one of my favourite Wimbledon champions.

If ever we needed an example of a young person who **appeared** to be troubled, we need look no further. I doubt if he would agree and would perhaps find it patronising but, to me, he has matured and emerged, like a butterfly from a chrysalis, into the much-loved figure he is today. His commentary at the annual championships shows not just his consummate knowledge of the game but, especially, from my point of view, that he is someone who can show that endearing quality of being able to smile at his former 'self.'

Chapter Ten

To Conclude

It may be that you have found countless examples of inspiration.

If we are open to suggestion, there will be a continuous stream of positivity with opportunities to read, hear, watch, experience, witness something which we find truly inspirational.

The experiences will no doubt be different for different people. But whatever it is that finds its way into your inner consciousness, it can take you into a new sense of wellbeing, optimism, motivation, determination or clarity, enabling you to think and/or act in a different way as a result.

It could be through listening to a piece of music, watching a film, or reading a particular book. Music in particular can stir our senses and elevate our mood by enabling us to relive a certain time and or place which has precious memories for us. Delius's 'On Hearing the First Cuckoo in Spring' or Vaughan Williams's 'The Lark Ascending', I believe are examples of two such pieces.

Just being in the presence of someone with whom we can identify – someone who can 'show us the way' can help us to answer the myriad of questions which has constantly plagued us.

A demonstration of the latter is very obvious in the case of teenagers, searching for they're not sure what but sure it has to be something different from what an older generation has settled for, seeking out likeminded souls amongst their peer group.

Even if they are solitary creatures, they may find their soul mate in the form of a musical artist to help them to come alive. How can this person, that they have never met, voice what could be their inner thoughts, their own words, as not even a loved family member is able to do at this stage? It's a wonderful, miraculous consolation.

They are searching for the image which they feel fits them and which will, even if it doesn't make them appear attractive to others, make them at least **noticed.**

Their destiny is not yet apparent and their image will probably change countless times, as they mature. We can do the same at whatever age.

If you believe that your destiny has not been decided for you – not by the sun, moon, stars or fate, and that a lot of the things that happen to us in life are purely accidental, then you may consider that your destiny is ultimately determined by **YOU.** It is ultimately determined by how you react to the situations you encounter in your life.

The Greek myth of Narcissus relates the story of how he fell in love with his own reflection in the water. There is a link here with depression, although not by way of vanity, but by way of self-absorption. It **may** be that one might have an excessive interest in one's physical appearance, but it is more that **whatever** you focus on intently can magnify and this becomes worse if you add self-disgust.

SO:

Try to take just small steps as you negotiate the path of the rest of your life whenever you are unsure of the way. Take care and control of what you tell your inner self – be gentle rather than harshly critical.

One of the most important lessons in life is to **hate no-one.** Hate can take over your life. You can waste your whole life by being dominated by the hatred for this person(s). How can you live a productive life in this manner? If not dealt with early on it can kill, one day at a time. Let go of this anger, let go of this person's domination of your life. Even if you can't forgive, leave it to other people in life to balance the scales.

You may find the following well known quotation, to be full of wisdom – I've chosen it to close my book.

Go placidly amid the noise and the haste, and remember what peace there may be in silence. As far as possible, without surrender, be on good terms with all persons. Speak your truth quietly and clearly; and listen to others, even to the dull and the ignorant; they too have their story. Avoid loud and aggressive persons; they are vexatious to the spirit. If you compare yourself with others, you may become vain or bitter, for always there will be greater and lesser persons than yourself. Enjoy your achievements as well as your plans. Keep interested in your own career, however humble; it is a real possession in the changing fortunes of time. Exercise caution in your business affairs, for the world is full of trickery. But let this not blind you to what virtue there is; many persons strive for high ideals, and everywhere life is full of heroism. Be yourself. Especially do not feign affection. Neither be cynical about love; for in the face of all aridity and disenchantment it is as perennial as the grass. Take kindly the counsel of the years, gracefully surrendering the things of youth. Nurture strength of spirit to shield you in sudden misfortune. But do not distress yourself with dark imaginings. Many fears are born of fatigue and loneliness. Beyond a wholesome discipline, be gentle with yourself. You are a child of the universe no less than the trees and the stars; you have a right to be here. And whether or not it is clear to you, no doubt the universe is unfolding as it should. Therefore, be at peace with God, whatever you conceive Him to be. And whatever your labours and aspirations, in the noisy confusion of life, keep peace in your soul. With all its sham, drudgery and broken dreams, it is still a beautiful world. Be cheerful. Strive to be happy.

Max Ehrmann, 1948

CONTACTS AND ORGANISATIONS FOR SUPPORT

If you visit **www.nhsuk mental health and wellbeing/mental health charities and organisations** you will find contact information for a variety of organisations offering support such as:

Depression Alliance

MIND

CRUSE Bereavement Care

Bipolar UK

CALM

No Panic

OCD UK

Samaritans

SANE

The Manic Depression Fellowship

and many others which may be particularly relevant to yourself.

There is also a variety of excellent Self-Help Books – browse them selectively, don't automatically select one written by a celebrity you admire. Try to find one or two which resonate with your own problems and thoughts, perhaps by a user-friendly psychologist.

Your notes